HOW TO BECOME

CEO

HOW TO BECOME

CEO

*The Rules
for Rising
to the Top
of Any
Organization*

JEFFREY J. FOX

VERMILION
LONDON

5 7 9 10 8 6

First published in the United States by Hyperion
Published by arrangement with Doris S. Michaels Literary Agency

First published in the United Kingdom in 2000 by Vermilion
an imprint of Ebury Press
Random House, 20 Vauxhall Bridge Road, London SW1V 2SA

Random House Australia (Pty) Limited
20 Alfred Street, Milsons Point, Sydney,
New South Wales 2061, Australia

Random House New Zealand Limited
18 Poland Road, Glenfield,
Auckland 10, New Zealand

Random House South Africa (Pty) Limited
Endulini, 5A Jubilee Road,
Parktown 2193, South Africa

The Random House Group Limited Reg. No. 954009
www.randomhouse.co.uk

A CIP catalogue record for this book is available from the British Library

ISBN 0 09 182661 6

Printed and bound in Great Britain by
Mackays of Chatham plc, Chatham, Kent

Papers used by Vermilion are natural, recyclable products
made from wood grown in sustainable forests.

Designed by Nicola Ferguson

To Legh F. Knowles, Jr.

(1919–1997)

Chairman of the Board

Beaulieu Vineyard

Napa, California

Musician — trumpet player in the Glenn Miller
Orchestra—super salesman,
quintessential CEO, mentor.

CONTENTS

{ vii }

CONTENTS

CONTENTS

CONTENTS

CONTENTS

CONTENTS

CONTENTS

CONTENTS

CONTENTS

CONTENTS

CONTENTS

INTRODUCTION

Why You Should Read
This Book

If you bought this book, you are ambitious. If someone gave you the book, that person thinks you are ambitious. Having ambition to better yourself, to be a contributor, to make a difference, to grow professionally, to be more successful, or to become CEO of an organization is good. CEO is the acronym for Chief Executive Officer. The CEO is the person who has strategic responsibility for the fortune and the future of the organization. The

CEO may be called Headmistress, Managing Partner, General of the Armies, Pontiff, Commander-in-Chief, Queen, or Warden. But whatever the title, the CEO is the boss. If becoming the boss is what you want, this book will help.

There are oodles of factors that influence the path to CEO—work habits, luck, timing, competitors, personality, supporters, talent, circumstances, and so on. This book will help you better your work habits, influence the odds, impact timing, surpass competitors, and deftly use your talent.

This is a book of advice and recommendations. The ideas are based on the realities of business and organizations. The ideas in this book are not a part of any MBA curriculum. They are crisp, blunt, frank, generally nonjudgmental, and easy to read, digest, and do.

Many of the recommendations are stated in rule or commandment form. This is because what is written is the way it is . . . not the way it ought to be. Although the content of the book is intended to help you progress in a company, the observations and advice are often applicable to your non-work life and activities, as well.

The surest way to become president or CEO of a corporation is to buy a business or to start a business. If you plan to make your career in a large corporation, this book will help. Of course, if you would rather run your own business, this book will also help.

This book has been skillfully edited by Laurie Abkemeier at Hyperion and is represented by the Doris S. Michaels Literary Agency, Inc. in New York. I am interested in your comments, thoughts, additions, and in any positive examples of your using the guidelines in this book. Write to me c/o Hyperion, 114 Fifth Avenue, New York, New York 10011.

Thank you.
—Jeffrey J. Fox

· I ·

Always Take the Job
That Offers the Most Money

After you have decided what you want to do—whether it is banking, advertising, manufacturing, or something else—go to work for the company that offers you the most money. If you have not decided what kind of career or industry is for you, then take the job that offers the most money. If you are in a corporation, always take the transfer, promotion, or assignment that pays the most money.

There are several important reasons why you go for the money. First, all of your benefits, perquisites, bonuses, and subsequent raises will be based on your salary. Corporations give all extra compensation in percentages. Therefore, a 10 percent raise on a £22,000 salary is £200 better than the same raise on a £20,000 salary.

Second, the higher paid you are, the more visible to top management you will be.

Third, the more money you are paid, the more contribution will be expected of you. This means you will be given more responsibility, tasks, and problems to solve. And a chance to perform is an invitation to success.

Fourth, if two people are candidates for a promotion to a job that pays £50,000, and one person makes £30,000 and the other £40,000 the higher paid person always gets the job. The higher paid person gets the job regardless of talent, contribution, or anything else. Corporations usually take the easy way out, and it is easier to promote the higher paid than the lower.*

Finally, in business, money is the scoreboard. The more you make, the better you're doing. Simple.

---

*Promoting the higher paid is the path of no resistance in most organizations. Someone approved the higher paid person's compensation. Others concurred. To leapfrog the higher paid diminishes the sponsor of the higher paid. And the sponsors of the higher paid are, themselves, even higher paid. Promoting the higher paid endorses the wisdom of upper management.

• II •
Avoid Staff Jobs,
Seek Line Jobs

*L*ine jobs make money for your corporation. Line jobs bring in money or have direct relationship with profits and loss.

The distinction between line and staff is sometimes blurred in corporations, but line jobs are where the action is.

Line jobs include salespeople, sales managers, product managers, plant managers, marketing directors, foremen, supervisors, and general managers. Staff jobs include lawyers, planners, data processing people, research and development scientists, and administrators of all types. Line jobs directly help the company get and keep customers. Legitimate staff jobs indirectly get and keep customers. Jobs that don't get and keep customers are redundant.

In most companies, most of the people are either in administration or in field sales. Administrative people are not bad, nor untalented. But they are not at the cutting edge. The company doesn't depend on them.

Take a staff job only if it is clearly temporary, a stepping stone, and if it pays more money.

Be sure you know what the line and staff jobs in your company are. Be sure to get the right one.

• III •

Don't Expect the Personnel Department to Plan Your Career

A mazingly, many managers think the Personnel department (a.k.a. Human Resources) is supposed to construct a career path for them. They think companies actually have a grand plan for them. Some managers think there is some kind of preordained job ladder as in the army or a police department. A young manager does basic training and the omniscient corporation promotes him or her to the next level up the pyramid.

It doesn't work that way.

Corporations don't have career plans for future presidents. It is doubtful if they have them for anybody. Your destiny and your career growth are your responsibility, no one else's. You have to know what you want. You have to design the plan to get there. You have to determine what skills and functional expertise are needed to get to the top in your company. Your responsibility is to acquire that experience.

· IV ·

Get and Keep
Customers

Customers are the lifeblood of any company. Everybody should know this. Everybody says "the customer is king" and "we work for the customer" and "the customer is the real boss." But very few employees in a corporation do anything to demonstrate they believe in this dictum. Commonly, the higher an executive gets, and the bigger the company, the less they deal with real honest-to-goodness existing and potential customers.

Executives reorganize companies, eliminate jobs, and excuse the chaos by saying they are "two or three levels closer to the customer." Bunk! There are no barriers between anyone in the corporation and the customer.

Why do so few people really work to get and keep customers? Because dealing with customers is tough. Customers reject sellers, they negotiate, they make harsh demands, they expect their needs to be filled, and they can be fickle. Also, dealing with administrative functions is an easier, impersonal, and safe task.

You must deal with today's customers *and* tomorrow's customers. They provide the ideas for new products and new applications. They provide the early warning signals about your products' quality and timeliness. They know about your competitors. To know your customers is to know your future.

When the phone rings twelve people ought to dive to answer it.

The customer is indeed king. And the future president understands how the customer is also the "king maker."

• V •

Keep Physically Fit

Your brain will make you money, but your body carries your brain. The better your physical condition, the greater your capacity for productive, unrelenting work.

And being in good condition gives you another edge. Ninety percent of all people climbing the corporate ladder are out of shape. You will be able to start earlier, pause less often, and end your day with a wind sprint.

You will also sleep better. You will be energetic and tire rarely. Your spirits will be up, and you will not get depressed.

You will have the energy and motivation to—at night and on weekends—coach soccer, attend the theater, volunteer.

How you keep fit is up to you.

· VI ·

Do Something Hard and Lonely

Regularly practice something Spartan and individualistic. Do something that you know very few other people are willing to do. This will give you a feeling of toughness, a certain self-elitism. It will mentally prepare you for the battle of business.

Something that is hard and lonely is studying late at night for a graduate degree in fashion design, especially in the winter, when everyone else is asleep. Or running long, slow distances early in the morning (versus jogging at lunchtime with a mob).

Split wood, write, work in the garden, read *King Lear*, but do it by yourself. Do something that is solitary.

All great and successful athletes remember the endless hours of seemingly unrewarded toil. So do corporate presidents.

• VII •

Never Write a Nasty Memo

Never write a memo that criticizes, belittles, degrades, or is hurtful to a colleague. Never write a memo that is cynical, condescending, or unkind. Never send a memo written in anger or frustration.

The world of business is very small. People get promoted, change companies, change jobs, have powerful friends, and do all of this around the world and throughout your forty- to fifty-year career. Companies merge, acquire, and get acquired. Your self-made enemy could show up anywhere.

Never give a company rival a smoking gun. Spend your energy on positive things.

• VIII •

Think for One Hour
Every Day

*S*pend one hard hour every day planning, dreaming, scheming, thinking, calculating. Review your goals. Consider options. Ponder problems. Write down ideas. Mentally practice your sales call or big presentation. Figure out how to get things done. Take mental stock.

Do this every day. Do it at a scheduled time. Do it at a desk or working table. Do not do it while driving or jogging. Don't do it while shaving or showering. Don't plan on this kind of thinking at work; you will be interrupted.

Keep written notes in your special "idea notebook."

• IX •

Keep and Use
a Special "Idea Notebook"

*B*uy a notebook you like. Keep it in one place—
in a desk drawer or in a briefcase pocket—
and leave it there. Write down all your ideas,
plans, goals, and dreams.

Use this notebook as the source for your
yearly, monthly, weekly, and daily "To Do" lists.
Good ideas always have their time. When they do,
commit them to action via your "To Do" list.

• X •

Don't Have a Drink
with the Gang

Don't have a drink with the "gang" after
work. It is a waste of time and money. Have
a drink with your spouse or with a friend.

Don't drink at lunch. Better, don't eat lunch.
Play squash or work.

When you're on the road at a sales meeting,
or a seminar, or a management meeting, don't go
to the cocktail party before dinner. Go running or

swimming instead. Have a sauna, shower, and dress for dinner.

Never get tipsy with anyone connected with your company. It is a sign of weakness. It shows you are out of control.

Don't Smoke

Nothing good happens to the people around you when you smoke cigarettes. You run a big risk of offending a nonsmoker who can help or hurt your career. Even smokers dislike the smoke and ashes and butts and dirty ashtrays and smell of smokers.

In addition to all the well-known, well-publicized arguments against smoking, there are other specific business reasons not to do so. Smoking wastes time. Smoking is a self-centered interest.

To get ahead in business you have to think of others, their needs and wants, not yours. Smoking interferes.

Cigarette smokers are, or appear to be, controlled. Winners in business are in control.

Smoking cigars is OK . . . if you are alone or with friends. Smoking an expensive cigar in the purview of a corporate chieftain is a mistake. The corporate chieftain will see you as pompous, as self-important, as having or spending too much money. If the boss gives you a celebration cigar, save it. You probably haven't yet earned the right to smoke a victory cigar.

• XII •

Skip All Office Parties

*T*here is no such thing as a business or "office party." It is not a social gathering. It is business. Never party at an office party. It won't hurt you not to go at all. Don't offend people by criticizing the party or by publicly announcing your intentions. Simply don't go. Give polite excuses.

Never ever go to a company picnic if you cannot bring your spouse. A company picnic without spouses is trouble. To go is to run the risk of being tarred with the bad brush of others' actions.

If the unwritten rule is "you must attend or you will offend" then go. Drink only soda. Stay no more than forty-five minutes. Thank the boss for inviting you, and leave. If anyone asks where you are going, tell that person you are meeting your spouse, or parents, or fiancée, or doctor, or music teacher, or personal trainer.

Parties are supposed to be fun, enjoyed with friends. Heed the old axiom: "Don't mix business with pleasure."

• XIII •
Friday Is
"How Ya' Doin'?" Day

*E*very Friday, take one of the people you need out to lunch and ask, "How ya' doin'?" These are usually people not in your department. They are important gears in the machine: people who help get your job done. If you're in sales, it is probably the sales manager's assistant, or the person who figures quotas, or someone who figures price quotes. If you're in marketing, it is someone in manufacturing, or R&D, or anywhere. If you are anywhere, there is always someone.

If you don't know who you need, find out. Business is like a machine. Every part needs to work. Every part needs to be oiled. Find out who you need, no matter how low in the organization, and let them know you know you need and appreciate them.

Make one good ally in your company every month.

• XIV •

Make Allies of Your Peers' Subordinates

Your peers are rivals for your next spot. The support of your peers' teammates is important. Their support of you will help you get your job done even if your peer deliberately or unintentionally acts to scuttle you. If your peer speaks well of you, her people will feel good because they already think the same. If your peer speaks poorly of you, her people will distrust her, or think less of her, because they think well of you.

• XV •

Know Everybody by Their First Name

To most people, there is no sound sweeter than their name remembered and pronounced correctly. Learn everybody's full name, and know something about them. Find out what they do and why their job is important. If you learn that, and you learn it sincerely, and the people know you know it, you will be successful.

A very good technique is to take visitors (customers, job candidates, friends) on an office or plant tour. Introduce them to people, telling the visitor what it is these other folks do that is important to the corporation.

Your coworkers will appreciate the acknowledgment and will be flattered that you have invested the energy to recognize and value who they are and what they do.

• XVI •

Organize "One-Line, Good-Job" Tours

*E*very once in a while get the highest ranking person you can to tour and visit your department. Before the tour write out a single 3" x 5" index card for every person. On the card write a one- or two-line report of some achievement or contribution—business or personal—that the person made. Use the cards as "cue cards" for the top guy, so that he can personally and specifically thank and compliment each person.

Everybody wins on a "good job" tour. The top guy will enjoy the natural positive feedback from your people, and he or she will be more informed. Your people will love the recognition and will be more motivated knowing they are appreciated. You will look very good. The collective positives of your people will be your accomplishment.

Don't let anybody in the company know you do this.

· XVII ·

Make One More Call

*T*ed Williams and Joe DiMaggio—two of the greatest hitters in baseball history—*each* took more batting practice than did all their teammates combined. It took Alexander Graham Bell over a thousand experiments to fashion a commercially viable phone prototype.

The difference between the successful person and the average is inches. The salesperson who makes one more sales call, the copywriter who does one more draft, the carpenter who nails one more board, the market researcher who does one more interview is going to be the best.

• XVIII •

Arrive Forty-five Minutes Early and Leave Fifteen Minutes Late

*I*f you are going to be first in your corporation, start practicing by being first on the job. People who arrive at work late don't like their jobs . . . at least that's what senior management thinks. People don't arrive twelve minutes late for the movies. And being early always gives you a psychological edge over the others in your company.

Don't stay at the office until ten o'clock every night. You are sending a signal that you can't keep up or that your personal life is poor. Leave fifteen minutes late instead. In those fifteen minutes organize your next day and clean your desk. You will be leaving after 95 percent of the employees anyway, so your reputation as a hard worker stays intact.

There are too many times in your career when circumstances such as airline schedules and sales meetings and year-end closings and such will keep you away from home until late. Give more time to your family.

Plus forty-five minutes early and fifteen minutes late is an hour a day. That's two hundred fifty hours a year or 31 days. You can get ahead quickly working one extra month a year.

· XIX ·

Don't Take Work Home
from the Office

Your home hours are for listening to your family, studying, planning, expanding your interests, and pitching batting practice to your kids. If you always have to take work home you are: (a) not managing your time properly; (b) boring; (c) wasting your precious nonwork hours; and (d) all of the above.

A very busy, and very good, advertising executive was always bringing home tons of work. Her elementary-school-age daughter, noting all the extra work her mother felt compelled to do, asked her innocently, "Mom, maybe you belong in a slower group?"

It is de rigueur for executives to take work home. But except for the reading of unimportant memos and ancient history (a.k.a. monthly reports), no real work is ever done. Your senior management may note you don't take work home (even though you do bring your briefcase) and decide to give you more projects and responsibility. And that's good.

• XX •

Earn Your
"Invitation Credentials"

*I*n every corporation there is, at the top, a *cosa nostra*, an inner, special family. This is the group that ultimately decides on who becomes CEO and for how long he will be in office. You must be invited into this inner group. You cannot simply work your way in or earn your way in with outstanding contributions. You must have more than talent. You have to acquire the same credentials that characterize those in the inner circle.

These characteristics are usually different in every corporation. In some corporations all the top people were salespeople early in their careers, or worked in a favored division, or were there ''at the beginning,'' or are Jewish or Boston Brahmin, or members of the founding family.

Find out who is in the inner circle. Find out why they are. Determine the necessary credentials. If the credentials are impossible to acquire, judge whether they might accept a token outsider (they often do). If you can't ever get the credentials, go to a corporation where you can.

If the top bank executives are all ex–loan officers, be sure to serve a stint making loans. If everyone in the executive suite is an engineer, you'd better be an engineer. If the top people were once salespeople, then carry the bag.

You can become CEO of the organization without being invited in, but you won't last. You will be kicked out in three to five years by either a powerful manager, a large shareholder, or by the ruling clique of the board of directors.

· XXI ·

Avoid Superiors
When You Travel

*M*ost people striving to climb the corporate ladder leap at the chance to travel with the top company executives. They think regaling the chairman or president or whomever with their latest project success and showing how bright they are is the way to the top. Don't do it. Good top managers judge on results, not clever conversation. Good top managers are also very busy, and unless you are working on one of their projects, after ten minutes, they want to spend their time on anything but you.

You should spend your travel time working. Airplane time is work time, so fly by yourself. If you travel with a top corporate executive and you spend the entire time working (as you must), he or she might think you are doing it for their benefit. Or worse, if they nap or read the airline magazine, and are even a little bit insecure, they will be unsettled by your industriousness. If you must fly on the same plane, sit in a different section.

Hotel time is also work time. If you travel with superiors they may feel obligated to ask you to dinner. If they don't, you'll feel hurt. Either way you waste valuable work time.

• XXII •

Eat in Your Hotel Room

Because you should be traveling alone, and because you spend your business day with customers or on other company affairs, you should have nights free. (If you do have a business dinner be sure you get some business done. Have an objective for the dinner and work to achieve it.) Spend your nights away from home, family, and friends working. Have dinner in your room. Get things done. Finish reports, read research papers, write memos, check your e-mail, complete expense accounts.

Dinner in your room saves time and money. It strengthens your individuality. It stretches your workday and extends your office. Spread your projects out, flick on a ballgame or a movie, order a bottle of Beaulieu Vineyard's cabernet sauvignon with dinner, and get some work finished.

Have breakfast in your room. Arrange for an exact service time. Get up early, do your exercises, get dressed, and start working. Don't waste time in a breakfast line with a hundred business people. Don't read the local newspaper. If you do business in another time zone which is open, call them. Plan your day. Set your daily objectives. Write your e-mail. Get some things done.

If you have a breakfast meeting (and these are excellent meetings) have an objective and an agenda, and work to achieve it.

· XXIII ·

Work, Don't Read Paperbacks, on the Airplane

Airplane travel is tough. It is crowded, interruptive, and hurried. Inbound telephone calls are rare on an airplane. No one will bug you. Plan your work according to the time aloft. Bring work easily managed on an airplane. Carry a small stapler. Bring a large prestamped envelope to send back to your office. Bring several envelopes and stamps to handle handwritten follow-up notes. Have a specific work objective for each trip.

• XXIV •

Keep a "People File"

Get a good, big address book or a notebook computer. From the first day on the job start keeping a file of all the people you meet, work with, and get to know. Be sure to note in your book what the people do: management recruiter, brand manager, printing supplier, freelance writer. Use pencil for your address book, as people change jobs and numbers constantly.

Every six months send a note to the people you don't see regularly—classmates, ex-colleagues, and so forth. Always ask people for their business card; inevitably they will ask for yours. Now you are in their file. Keep a backup copy of your "people file" in a safe place. Use this file during your entire career.

Do this simple act of "people linkage." No one else will do it quite the same way. Invest in people (see chapter XXXVIII).

• XXV •

Send Handwritten Notes

*I*mpersonal communication pervades. There is fax mail, e-mail, junk mail, voice mail, talk-and-type computers, pagers, beepers, PINs, ATMs, talking car doors, digitized wake-up calls. Greeting cards are prewritten for you. No one composes their own "roses are red, violets are blue" Valentine's Day cards.

Handwritten notes stand out. They are digitalis for the digital world. They will differentiate you, mark you as a person of manners and merit. They are personal, of the gracious past, and never out of style.

There are endless occasions that warrant a handwritten note: thank-yous, praise, congratulations, regrets, for your information, thought you'd like to know, your presentation was just great, and your cassoulet was world class.

Go to a good stationery store. Order a box of exceptional quality cards and envelopes . . . with your name on the cards and your address on the envelopes. Keep the box in your desk, and carry some in your briefcase.

Send one handwritten note a week . . . for starters.

• XXVI •

Don't Get Buddy-Buddy with Your Superiors

You and your superiors are business associates. You are not friends. There is a necessary line between you. Don't cross it and get buddy-buddy. Don't let your superiors cross it either. A lot of people think that becoming personal friends with senior executives is smart, and they work at it. They contrive meetings, seek invitations to the same parties, join the same country clubs, and all the rest. This is not the foundation for a successful career. It is a substitution for talent. And it is obvious.

Do get to know your boss and her bosses very well. Know their problems, plans, personalities, idiosyncrasies, weaknesses, strengths, and everything else. Always be there to help, both in business and personally. But toe the friendship line. You can become friends later when you are in different companies.

Same thing goes for your subordinates.

• XXVII •

Don't Hide an Elephant

*B*ig problems always surface. If they have been hidden, even unintentionally, the negative fallout is always worse. The "hiders" always get burned, regardless of complicity. The "discoverers" always are safe, regardless of complicity. When you know there is a problem, a goof, a snafu, and it is important, let your supervisors and colleagues know right away. The longer you wait the more you increase the severity of the problem.

You can turn a big problem into an opportunity to shine. Define and explain the problem carefully. Give estimates of potential damage. Describe possible scenarios. Suggest some solution options. Ask for help. This is important. It is also very important to position yourself as an independent reporter, in control. Describe the problem and treat it as if you were not previously involved. Loosen entanglements.

Watergate, Vietnam, and surprise business bankruptcies are classic elephants, apparently well hidden, that were mismanaged and produced disastrous results. Each elephant grew with the hormones of panic and deception. The crisis managers were like children trying to save sandcastles from the tide. Note, however, how President John F. Kennedy handled his Bay of Pigs debacle. Preemptively, publicly, on television, "my fault, we blew it, any questions?" Kennedy emerged unscathed, actually strengthened.

• XXVIII •

Be Visible:
Practice "WACADAD"

Promote yourself within the corporation. Do so by working on projects that are visible or are the pet projects of senior people. Ask people what the big problems are. Think about them. Work on solutions. Test them. Write up your proposals, and get proper distribution of your ideas.

Don't talk about how good you are. Prove it with action, over and over. Remember WACADAD. "Words are cheap and deeds are dear."

Ted Leavitt of Harvard Business School wrote that "creativity without implementation is irresponsibility." Ideas are nothing without execution.

So few people in a corporation actually execute ideas that the person who does becomes visible, and is often sought to do more.

Pick your spots to shine. Presentations to senior management, instructing a training class, and speaking before the sales force are highly visible forums. Seek them, and work very hard to prepare outstanding presentations.

· XXIX ·

Always Take Vacations

*T*he executive who brags she never takes vacations is either a fool or a poor manager. You must be able to establish your department, job, or area of responsibility so it can function smoothly without you. Otherwise you won't be able to travel to see customers.

There are several career reasons to take vacations. If you go to the right places you increase your chances of meeting people who have the potential to help you. It is an occasion to observe other ways of life, new fashions and trends, different ways business is done, and literally to broaden your horizons. It is the time to write a book or practice photography or sample the risottos of Tuscany. It is a time to think and plan. And, not unimportantly, a planned vacation forces you to work incredibly hard before you leave and finish lots of work.

Always plan your vacation far in advance. Pick your winter dates a year in advance. Let your superiors know well ahead of time. Never cancel. Never leave a telephone number. Experiment and go to different places. But always go.

• XXX •

Always Say "Yes" to a Senior Executive Request

The time management books will tell you this is wrong, that always saying "yes" weakens your control over time. But always say "I can do it" when a top guy asks. Even if he asks you to water the plants in the lobby, do it.

Listen carefully to the request. The guy might be suggesting a solution, not stating the core problem. However, what he really wants is the problem solved. Evaluate his solution to see if it fits the need. If not, provide a different solution, and get the real job done.

No matter what the request, give him more than he wanted, sooner than expected, and with your own touch of personal innovation.

People who get the job done are the ones who get the top jobs.

• XXXI •

Never Surprise Your Boss

Bosses don't like surprises. They get enough unknowns from the business environment, their supervisors, cunning rivals, and other subordinates. They don't need surprises—good or bad—from you. They want to be informed. They want to be able to answer their boss's question about the states of projects, progress on the latest crisis, and everything else. Your boss wants to appear in control, on top of things. It is a discourtesy to him, and to the organization, for you to keep your boss in the dark.

If you surprise your boss, he will begin to mistrust you. You must have the trust of your boss. Good or bad, he is there, and he usually has the most influence on your early career.

Your boss is often more informed about company events that don't concern you. A surprise, even if well-intentioned, when mixed with the wrong kind of unfolding events can be disastrous.

Put yourself in your boss's place. No surprises.

• XXXII •

Make Your Boss Look Good,
and Your Boss's Boss Look Better

Getting real promotions usually requires a vacancy up the ladder. Your best chance is to succeed your boss. But she can't get promoted unless there is someone to replace her. Making her look good improves her promotability, and because you make her look good she will want you to stay around. You are now promotable.

Your boss cannot promote you without getting approval from her superiors. If you have made

your boss's boss look better your entire promotability equation will be enhanced. Your boss's boss
is always the key. He is often more interested and
influential in your career than your immediate superior. This is absolutely true if your boss is not
going anywhere.

You make these people look good by antici-
pating their needs and problems and by doing the
extra work needed to get answers. Always keep
them informed. Always finish work ahead of schedule. Always do a bit more. See their job through
their eyes. Help them by doing the project and
making suggestions as if you were in their place.
Don't let them make a mistake.

· XXXIII ·

Never Let a Good Boss
Make a Mistake

One of the best things that can happen to you to help your ascendancy in a corporation is to work for a good boss. A good boss trains you to take her place, and when she ultimately gets promoted, you have a chance to progress.

Don't let your good boss make a mistake that could hurt her promotability, because that directly hurts your promotion chances. Don't let your good boss make a mistake that could hurt your company, because that makes it harder for the company to flourish . . . and the better your company performs, the more resources are available for rewards.

If your boss needs more facts to make a decision, do her homework. If your boss is ill prepared for a meeting, give her a heads-up briefing. If your boss has a weak presentation, beef it up.

Don't link the potential mistake with your boss personally. Don't say, "*You* are making a mistake," or "There is an error in *your* report." Handle the mistake avoidance like this: "Mary, there may be a problem in *this* budget. It looks like *the* cost numbers are understated. If *we* use ten dollars an hour for the rate instead of eight *we* will have a more realistic budget."

Corollary: Tell everyone who works for you— inside and outside the organization—that they must never let you make a mistake. Be sure your boss knows you have that rule.

• XXXIV •

Go to the Library
One Day a Month

*L*eave the office and take one workday a month, or every three weeks, and go to a local public or university library. Commandeer a big work table, and organize all your "to do" projects. Knock off all the detailed stuff. Get the administrivia finished.* Organize your big projects into small, di-

---

*Administrivia describes those little business tasks, such as paperwork, expense accounts, report reviews, that, if not completed, can cause big problems.

gestible pieces. Get your people file up to date. Organize your idea book. Write all your follow-up memos, customer letters, and thank-you notes.

One good, uninterrupted workday in a quiet library will enable you to accomplish ten times more than you could with the same number of hours in your office. The feeling of getting so much done will embolden you, give you a sense of being ahead, in control, and will motivate you to work hard on your regular responsibilities.

• XXXV •

Add One Big New Thing to Your Life Each Year

*T*o be qualified to be a chief executive officer of a corporation you must be broad-gauged, widely read, and have many diverse interests. You need to see solutions to your problems in the ways of other cultures, nature, music, how beavers build dams, anything. You also need to focus your energy and practice discipline.

Adding one new big permanent facet to your life will prepare you for the presidency of your corporation. Learn a foreign language, Chinese cooking, or photography. Write a book, raise orchids, or breed canaries. Learn to play "Blueberry Hill" on the piano.

Make a list of the things you want to do in the next ten years. Nothing you want to do should be omitted. When you say you are too old to learn tennis, you're saying you don't have the capacity to grow, expand, or run an enterprise. If you don't have the time, how will you ever get the time to handle a bigger job with twice the responsibility?

Demonstrate your ability to grow.

· XXXVI ·

Study These books

Obvious Adams by Robert Updegraff
Acres of Diamonds by Russell Conwell
The Bible
The Art of War by Sun-Tzu
The Book of Five Rings
   by Musashi Miyamoto
On War by Carl von Clausewitz
The Prince by Niccolò Machiavelli
Bartlett's Familiar Quotations
Webster's Third Unabridged Dictionary

The Forbes Book of Business Quotations
  Edited by Ted Goodman
The Complete Works of Shakespeare
On Advertising by David Ogilvy
The Sun Also Rises by Ernest Hemingway
The Elements of Style by William Strunk and
  E. B. White
Huckleberry Finn by Mark Twain
Anything by Thomas Jefferson

• XXXVII •

"Dress for a Dance"

A very wise high school principal once disagreed with a young student-council president who wanted to change the strict dress code for the sophomore dance: "Dress for football, you play football. Dress for a dance, you dance." The same lesson holds for business. Dress for business, you do business.

In some places, companies, and industries, different dress codes reflect different cultures. This is fine, and you should be hip to each culture. For example, in Puerto Rico and Hawaii business is often conducted in shirtsleeves. In the field, executives sometimes wear work boots and hard hats. Plant managers wear safety glasses and lab coats. These are easily understood exceptions.

Practice being presidential all the time, and that includes the business uniform. You don't have to spend a ton of money on tailored suits or become a fashion plate. Buy a book on how to dress in business, such as *John T. Molloy's New Dress for Success* or *New Women's Dress for Success* also by John T. Molloy, and note how successful people dress.

• XXXVIII •

Overinvest in People

*H*ire the best people. Attract, motivate, train, and reward the best people.

Companies that "save money" by only hiring people they can "afford" are headed to mediocrity in their industry . . . if they are not already there. It is better to hire one exceptional person at £60,000 than two average people at £25,000 each. Overinvest with emotional currency, as well. Give the winners trust, independence, praise, freedom, encouragement.

Leaders of organizations know that people make things happen. They never forget this elemental truth. Without an army, a general is nothing. If the people in your organization support you, trust you, believe in you, and respect you, they will propel you to the top. But the people in the organization give back only what they get. They are mirrorlike reflectors. If trusted, they trust back. If respected, they respect back. Many executives fail because the other employees know their leader is insincere, dishonest, fearful, or untrustworthy. People will accept intellectual, physical, cultural, even moral flaws in their leaders. But they will never accept an antipeople character.

Hire people according to the three "I's":

"I" for integrity. First priority.

"I" for the "I can do it" attitude. Critical.

"I" for intelligence. If the person knows what they don't know, or that they might have to work 10 percent harder than a Ph.D., that's intelligence enough.

Once you find this rare person, overinvest in her. She will know it and give you a great return on the investment.

People are not dumb. They are not in business to lose money or to make mistakes and enemies. All they need is a little wise investment.

• XXXIX •

Overpay Your People

*I*f a person should be paid £5.00 an hour she
knows it. If you pay her £4.75 it will cost you
a hundred times the savings in sabotage. She will
feel cheated. She won't go the extra inch, won't
work the extra hour. She will find a way—mentally, physically, or economically—to punish you
for paying her unfairly.

If a person should be paid £5,00, and everyone
knows it, pay her £5.75. You will get much more

production than the extra £.75 it will cost you, because the person will stretch to justify your confidence in her.

Shortsighted managers don't understand this. They think they are keeping costs down. They think people should be happy to have the job in the first place. They believe people aren't worth their pay. On an individual basis some people aren't worth their pay, and they can exist at any level in the organization. Get rid of them, for they take money from the real workers. One nonearner's salary can be spread among many.

You can't cut people costs and save money. People are an asset, a contributing return on investment. You make money on people. If an investment in a bank account was returning 20 percent on capital, would you cut costs (i.e., reduce your investment)? Of course not. You would increase your investment.

You are much better off to have fewer exceptional people all making more money than they should, than to have the same or lower payroll costs with more people.

• XL •

"Stop, Look, and Listen"

Presidents reflect. They don't shoot from the lip. They think, consider, ponder, observe, probe, and listen. They stop and observe. They stop before saying the wrong thing. They stop before making a snap decision. They stop before sending the barbed letter. And they watch and listen some more.

To become a president you must master the art of and ability to stop, look, and listen. Listening is very difficult, especially for aggressive, energetic, bright people. You must train yourself to always be on "high receive." You have to hear the unsaid, just as Sir Arthur Conan Doyle's Sherlock Holmes heard the dog that didn't bark. You have to listen to what the eyes, hands, and frowns are saying. You have to listen to customers, suppliers, supervisors, colleagues, noncustomers, company salespeople, competitors, everybody.

Listening can be learned. It can be practiced. When someone is speaking, stop what you are doing, look at the person, and listen. Good listeners are considered great conversationalists. Listening is equated with wisdom and intelligence.

Listen, listen, listen!

• XLI •

Be a Flag-Waving
Company Patriot

If you want to be president of your company, you must commit yourself totally to your company and to its products or services. You must understand and believe in your company's mission. You must personalize your company's culture, and then add to it. You must do this unflaggingly, publicly, and without reserve.

You must use the products, if possible, and promote them tirelessly to all.

Do not go to work for a company if you cannot, unabashedly, shout the virtues of their products. If you do not believe in smoking, handguns, champagne, or yogurt don't work for companies that make such stuff.

Buy stock in your company if it's available.

Only buy your company's products, if that is reasonable, and recommend them stridently to friends and family.

Cynicism about one's own corporation is the hallmark of losers, not future presidents.

· XLII ·

Find and Fill
the "Data Gaps"

*I*n business when someone says "I think" or
"we believe" or "it's my opinion" that means
they don't know. Identify what you don't know
and what your organization doesn't know. These
are "data gaps."

Don't be misled by the clever articulation of
bright people in the company who only talk to each
other and never leave the office. Get the facts. Talk
to customers and users.

People who know they cannot possibly know everything but are willing to work very hard to find the data succeed.

· XLIII ·

Homework, Homework, Homework

Most people in business never really work hard. They manufacture a busy look by bustle and busywork. They read reports, go to meetings, write long-winded memos, fill out forms, and waste time. This is the "rocking chair syndrome"—lots of movement, but they're not going anywhere.

Hard workers spend the same amount of time, but they use it intensely. They do the hard things.

They do the homework. They find out the facts. They figure out how to get something done. They work on the nitty-gritty details of execution. They cover all the bases and consider all the options. But most of all, they think. They dig.

The "rocking chair" guy prepares for his history test by reading eight chapters ten times in seven hours. The homework guy breaks the chapters apart, synthesizes the information, and memorizes the eight chapters in seven hours.

Success in projects is anticlimactic. Homework preordains it.

• XLIV •

Never Panic . . .

or Lose Your Temper

> Nothing gives one person so much advantage over another as to remain cool and unruffled under all circumstances.
>
> —THOMAS JEFFERSON

*T*emper tantrums, immobilization, unwise snap decisions, finger pointing, and acts of cowardice are all signs of panic. Good presidents don't panic. They don't throw tantrums. They keep themselves in control so they can keep control of the situation.

In the course of making fine wine, one of the crucial time periods is the crush. The crush is those few weeks when the grapes are selected for harvest, tested for quality, chosen or rejected, and crushed to release the juice that will eventually become wine. Mistakes or misjudgments during the crush can adversely impact the entire vintage resulting in a damaged reputation and reduced prices and profits.

Some years ago, in the midst of the crush at a famous winery, the president received a frantic call from his managers. The winemaker had resigned. The president instantly knew the damage potential, but he stayed calm, thought for some moments, then asked, "What would you do if the winemaker had died instead of resigned?" The managers said they would make so-and-so the winemaker. "So be it," said the president, and the new winemaker carried on the winery tradition for fifteen more years.

If a colleague makes an unkind comment to you, do not respond, but it is OK to laugh. Your supporters will be as offended as you. Your detractors will sense your control. Anyone else will see you as above the fray. Do not get angry. Even when anger is justified, observers are put off by the angry person.

School yourself not to panic. Tell yourself to "stay calm." If you have ten seconds to make a decision think for nine.

• XLV •

Learn to Speak and Write in Plain English

You must learn to communicate. You must be articulate. More time and money are lost in business due to poor communication than to any other reason. Billions of dollars in advertising is wasted annually. Billions of human hours are spent doing wrong or unnecessary tasks. Billions of pages of reading matter are never read.

Business communications must be precise, complete, and totally comprehensible. Both written and verbal communication, especially job direction, must be to the point. Long, tedious, flowery, jargon-filled communications are wasteful.

If your people don't get it right, they won't do it right. Spend as much time as necessary getting perfect mutual understanding of what is to be done. The irony about communication in industry is that so much is communicated about the lack of communication. Good communication is hard work. It requires a sensitivity to the audience or reader(s). You must understand your audience's needs, their mindsets, available time, and other priorities, how they absorb information, and their educational level.

Follow these guidelines for clear communication:

Be sure your letter or memo is necessary.
Have a specific objective for the communication.
Choose the simplest mode possible.
Do the homework, and have all the facts.

Write a scattergram of all your points.*
Organize the message carefully.
Write a zero draft.†
Write a first draft.
Edit ruthlessly to a one-page final draft.
Use language your audience will understand.

A good rule of thumb: think for three hours, write for one.

---

*A scattergram is a written collection of all the points, ideas, facts that will go into your writing. Don't prioritize or organize. This is a "get started" tool.
†A zero draft is your first attempt, and is always rewritten, condensed.

• XLVI •

Treat All People
as Special

*P*eople are more than people. They are indi-
viduals. They are mothers, fathers, soccer
coaches, charity workers, PTO volunteers, Sunday
school teachers, and contributors. They can do a
lot if it is appreciated, and they can do more if
they are motivated and thanked.

Excellent managers make people feel that they

are asked, not questioned . . .
are overpaid, not underpaid . . .
are measured, not monitored . . .
are people, not personnel . . .
are sold on what to do, not told . . .
are instrumental, not instruments . . .
are workers, not worked . . .
are contributors, not costs . . .
are needed, and heeded.

• XLVII •

Be a Credit Maker,
Not a Credit Taker

Give everybody 100 percent credit for the work they do. If you have five people reporting to you and each gets 100 percent, you get 500 percent. That's the way it works.

It's like building a house: 100 percent for the guy who puts in the foundation, 100 percent for the roofer, 100 percent for the electrician, and the contractor gets the sum of the parts.

Many managers don't understand this. They think if their people look too good, they'll be diminished. They think they have to have some of the credit, especially for the fantastic roof. So they steal it. They tell their boss, other superiors, colleagues, and even the guy who did the work that they were really responsible.

The credit taker is insecure, dishonest, and known to all. Even the cleverest credit taker is ultimately found out. He is found out first by the people who work under him. Then, albeit slowly, by the rest of the organization.

Give proper credit and you will become known as a credit maker, as somebody who gets things done, as a person to work for. Your people will work very hard, as they know they will be fairly recognized.

• XLVIII •

Give Informal
Surprise Bonuses

*I*f someone does an extraordinarily good job on
something, particularly something that is not
part of his regular responsibility, give him a bonus.
(Don't expect your company's compensation pol-
icy to allow this. It won't. Like all corporate policies, the one on compensation is designed to
dampen innovation.)

Don't publish criteria for your bonus system.
Don't even publish the bonus system itself, the

word will get around. Be irregular. Give different amounts at different times of the year.

Everyone who works for you will know that if they do a superlative job lightning might strike. And they will work hard to increase their chances.

· XLIX ·

Please, Be Polite
with Everyone

Use good manners, all the time, with everyone. Be gracious. Never pull rank. Never
wear your boss's stripes. Don't smoke in someone
else's office or car. Don't smoke at meetings or
meals. Don't swear or use coarse language. Don't
put your feet on office furniture. Don't put your
briefcase on a conference table. Treat your office,
everyone else's office, salespeople's cars, and all
company belongings as if they were yours.

Always be on time for appointments. Don't let salespeople or visitors wait in the lobby. Don't keep people holding on the phone. Be conscious of other people's time . . . don't waste it. Particularly don't waste your subordinates' time. Courtesy is good business.

Always introduce yourself, your spouse, and anyone else clearly and slowly. Always introduce your subordinates to the senior people in your organization.

Always say "please" and "thank you."

• L •

Ten Things to Say
That Make People Feel Good

People who feel good about themselves and their jobs will contribute at high levels. If they work for you, with you, or near you, they will propel you in front of them. Saying nice things to people makes them feel good. But you must be absolutely sincere. Practice and remember to say the following:

1. "Please."
2. "Thank you." (A good manager has cause to say "thank you" twenty times a day.)
3. "You remember Larry Kessler in our Accounts Payable department." (An introduction of someone to a superior.)
4. "That was a first-class job you did."
5. "I appreciate your effort."
6. "I hear nothing but good words about you."
7. "I am glad you are on the team."
8. "I need your help."
9. "You certainly earned and deserve this."
10. "Congratulations."

• LI •

The Glory and the Glamour
Come after the Gruntwork

Graduations, promotions, trophies, kudos, varsity letters, Salesperson of the Year awards, President's Club memberships, and such represent the glory and glamour. Corner offices and big money are also part of the glory and glamour. These are the visible parts of success in business. However, it is the invisible, day-to-day, behind-the-scenes toil and gruntwork that many people don't see, appreciate, or do.

It is the gruntwork that counts and begets the glory. It is the homework, the early mornings, the weekend travel away from home, the checking and rechecking, the trial and error, and the endless hours of inch-by-inch progress that the glamour masks.

If you begrudge the gruntwork you will not get the glory.

• LII •

Tinker, Tailor, Try

*I*n business, failure costs so much money that almost every satisfied company with more than a thousand employees avoids the risk of innovation. Perhaps 97 percent of all people in all organizations are afraid of change and innovation. But new ideas and new products are what create new customers and are the wellspring for a company's continued vitality and survival.

The ability to create new products is tedious, difficult, and, regardless of the company rhetoric, almost always counterculture. To be an innovator in corporations is unique, but it is a quality boards of directors seek.

Not many things work perfectly the first time. Hit novels and Broadway plays aren't published after one draft. New product development is a labyrinth of wrong routes and dead ends. Ideas need noodling and tinkering and fiddling to become workable.

Nurture the good idea. Spend a little, not a lot. Don't risk big money in the embryonic stage. Get feedback. Tinker with the concept. Tailor it to better fill the needs of the target audience. Most importantly, try something. Try this, try that. Don't talk, don't have meetings, don't write memos. Do something: make an ad concept, build a prototype, give out samples. Then tinker some more, tailor it a bit, and try again. If it's a bad idea, you'll know it. Drop it. If it's a good idea, you'll now be able to sell it to the corporation. You can manage the risk and manage the investment escalation.

· LIII ·

Haste Makes Waste

One business myth is that it is admirable to be the aggressive, super-sure, rapid-fire manager who makes one quick decision after another. This style might be OK if the decisions can be reversed or altered with little impact or if there is a catastrophe with an absolute time frame, such as a fire in the factory. But decisions made for speed's sake are risky.

There are two kinds of decisions: revocable and irrevocable. Knowing the difference is a hallmark of the good manager. Revocable decisions are changeable decisions and can be made relatively fast, because their impact is less and, if wrong, there is time to redo. The organization has to live with irrevocable decisions.

Learn what defines revocable and irrevocable in your organization. Here are typical examples of revocable decisions:

- Office layouts
- Advertising schedules
- Pricing
- Not making a decision
- Committee assignments
- Company policies
- Choosing an insurance company
- Phone services

Generally, these kinds of decisions are irrevocable:

- Brand names
- Acquisitions
- Executive hires
- Buildings
- Computer systems

You must always think fast and study fast to be able to decide fast.

• LIV •

Pour the Coals
to a Good Thing

*I*f you find a good thing, no matter how prosaic, old, or tried and true, pour the coals to it. Not every success is solving the big problem, developing the hot product, or turning around the bad division. The financial objective of an enterprise is to provide a significant return to the shareholders. You do this by the profitable finding and filling of customer needs. If the customers like it, don't change it. Don't change the label, the ingredients, the name, the price, the advertising, or anything else.

The Disney company understands a good thing. Mickey Mouse made his stage debut over fifty years ago. Understanding the phenomenal allure of Mickey Mouse, Disney invested heavily to create an American icon. And today Mickey Mouse greets kids in Disney World, stars in books and movies, sells everything from dolls to eyeglasses, and is the star of Disney stores.

Procter & Gamble never tires of telling people that Ivory soap is "99 and 44/100 percent pure." In fact, P&G has been using that slogan for over a hundred years, and Ivory soap continues to be one of the best selling soaps in the U.S.

Don't change the formula for success. Rather, pour the coals to it.

• LV •

Put the Importance on the Bright Idea, Not the Source of the Idea

*A*lways be on the lookout for ideas. Be completely indiscriminate as to the source. Get ideas from customers, children, competitors, other industries, or cab drivers. It doesn't matter who thought of an idea. What matters is who implements the idea.

Many managers don't understand this.

Creative people are doers. They recognize a good idea right away. They add their own personality in the relentless execution of the idea.

Creative people don't say, "Whose brilliant idea was that?" They don't belittle ideas or the suggesters. They can't be bothered.

Truly creative people realize they have only one brain, no matter how fertile. So they enhance the probability of getting good ideas by listening to the ideas of others. If they listen to one hundred people, they've multiplied their creative capacity one hundred times.

• LVI •

Stay Out of Office Politics

So many executives think the road to the top is paved with the bodies of their colleagues. They scheme to embarrass or downgrade their fellow managers. The crude ones are gunslingers, the clever ones use stilettos. They are often sycophants. They are at your feet or at your throat. They are obvious. They survive only in poor organizations.

Rampant office politics is symptomatic of a weak leader. The reward system is probably not fair or clear. The fiefdom may even be in trouble. Instead of fighting the competition or crusading for new customers, the executives fight each other, try to curry favor, and waste time.

Don't waste your time. Spend your time creating and accomplishing. Let your actions be your politics. In good companies, contribution counts.

Be the last to know. Don't get sucked in. Don't let people tell you something if they say it's "confidential." Don't ask, don't answer, don't agree. Don't say anything bad about anyone. Don't gossip. Say, "I don't know."

Just work.

• LVII •

Look Sharp and Be Sharp

A little vanity is good. Look after yourself, and keep an attractive appearance. Stay trim. Get your hair cut properly. Avoid garish and faddish and cheap quality clothes. Maintain a healthy outdoors look. Get rid of the jailhouse pallor.

Don't be sickly. Think healthy. Take vitamins. Exercise and eat properly. Recognize unhealthy stress, and find ways to relax and reduce stress. Get an annual physical.

Have a bright smile. Brush your teeth, and have fresh breath. Get your teeth fixed, and get braces if you need them. Keep your hair, hands, and fingernails clean. Eliminate dandruff, and avoid heavy cologne.

Polish your shoes regularly. Put a fresh flower in your lapel, if you wish. Put a lilt in your step.

Be up. And smile.

• LVIII •

Emulate, Study, and Cherish the Great Boss

*M*ost people can count their memorable teachers, from kindergarten through graduate school, on one hand. The same is true with coaches and mentors. It is particularly true in business. Great bosses are not common. There are lots of nice people, and there are a few disasters. But the great boss is a rarity.

He or she teaches without preaching. They praise properly. The great bosses are challenging and fair goal setters. They are honest. They let their people grow without the restraints of harsh judgment, public criticism, or corporate bureaucracy. Some may be idiosyncratic and have whims, even touches of pettiness. But they are always experienced, hardworking, open-minded, and smart.

Seek those people out early in your career. Work for them. Watch them closely. See how they handle criticism and problems. Note how they manage people. Find out how they get things done.

Learn their way.

• LIX •

Don't Go Over Budget

Get your job done on time and within budget. Senior managers promote people who deliver what is expected. Exceeding budget causes problems. Businesses are always under pressure to reduce costs. Budget overages intensify the pressure.

Do not be like the U.S. Congress or state highway departments. Even on the smallest scale in a corporation there is a need to stay within budget. The burden on the manager is to know clearly what his objectives are and to plan and price the execution carefully.

Tight budgets promote creativity, ingenuity, and inventiveness. Look upon a tight budget as a challenge. Find new and less expensive ways of doing things. The corporation will be improved. You will be appreciated.

· LX ·

Never Underestimate an Opponent

O pponents can be competitors, rival managers, or buying committees. They will come
in every physical form: man, woman, fat, trim,
old, young, nerdy, or charismatic. Opponents will
be articulate, bumblers, shufflers, or joggers. Do
not be misled by appearance or reputation. Do not
become overconfident or smug. Assume nothing.

Never underestimate an opponent's intelligence, stamina, or skill. Never underestimate their

capacity for good or evil, including duplicity, dishonesty, and cunning.

If you underestimate an opponent you may get knocked on your butt. If you overestimate an opponent you may be pleasantly surprised.

· LXI ·

Assassinate the Character Assassin
with a Single Phrase

One of the most dangerous impediments to one's career is the character assassin. The character assassin usually thrives in a firm racked by office politics. But he can be anywhere. He can be your boss. He is always dishonest, ambitious, and treacherous. The character assassin targets the up-and-comers. He goes after all potential rivals, but upward striving managers are likely victims because they tend to take more risks and make more mistakes.

The character assassin instinctively understands Mark Twain's brilliant observation on falsehood. Twain wrote in his essay "Advice to Youth" that the "truth is not hard to kill," but "a lie well told is immortal."

The character assassin is obvious and apparent to the keen observer, and he will and does attack everyone. These two traits are his vulnerability.

When conversation with a colleague turns to the character assassin, and it will, if you are a target, simply say, "Of course, with Mr. X, no one is spared."

Your colleague, knowing of Mr. X's style, will assume he, too, has been a recent target. Assassin assassinated.

· LXII ·

Become a Member
of the "Shouldn't Have Club"

People who belong to the "should've club" are always saying, "I should've done that"; "I could've done that"; or "I would've done that." The "should've club" is full of nondoers, the risk averse. They never go for it. They are so afraid of losing, they never plan to win.

The "should've club" is boring. The members never get cut or scratched. They never miss a shot in the last second. There are no reprimands, and they make no waves. There is not an Arnold Palmer or Chris Evert or Larry Bird in this club.

The "shouldn't have club" is the place to be. This is the winners' circle. Each time you admonish yourself with "Gee, I shouldn't have done that" there will be ten other times when the results will prove you should have.

No guts, no glory.

· LXIII ·

The Concept Doesn't Have to Be Perfect, but the Execution of It Does

*I*f you wait for the perfect time, for the perfect new product, for conditions to be just right, you will never get started. Even the greatest of companies and products have been improved since their beginning. If the concept is better than any-thing else, and it fills a need better than what's on the market now, then do it. If it's a better way, don't wait until it gets a little better. Do not let "perfect" be the enemy of "better."

Execute the concept's development and introduction with meticulous attention to detail. Leave nothing undone. Get the product out on time. Be sure the pricing, advertising, and everything else is right. No matter what you are trying to launch, from a new product to a new manufacturing process to a real estate development, it is the excellence of execution that will determine success or failure.

• LXIV •

Record and Collect Your Mistakes with Care and Pride

*M*istakes are milestones. They indicate action in new and unexperienced areas. They are learning devices. Keep track of them in a section of your idea notebook (see chapter IX). State exactly what you did wrong, where you made the wrong move, what motivated you to blow it. What prompted you to say the wrong thing? Were you angry, acting immature, gossiping, or bragging? Did you skip a step in the homework, ignore a seemingly minor detail, or were you lazy? Be your own Monday-morning quarterback.

Whatever the root cause of your mistake, record it. You probably will never make it again. Make notes on what you learned, how you would handle the same event again.

Acknowledging mistakes is a sign of security and confidence. It shows a willingness to try new things and take on uncertain ventures. Mistakes are the exhaust of active, doing people.

A record of mistakes is often the memorabilia of a very successful person.

• LXV •

Live for Today;
Plan for Tomorrow;
Forget about Yesterday

You can't bring back yesterday. So don't try. Don't brood over yesterday, and don't gloat. Get on with today. Today is very important. It is whatever you want it to be.

Plan for tomorrow. It will be a good day.

• LXVI •

Have Fun, Laugh

Business is tough enough not to have fun. If your job isn't fun, you have to change jobs or find ways to add some fun.

If you can make the jobs of others a lot of fun, they will work harder and more creatively and feel more satisfied with their careers and lives. A working environment that is constantly blood-and-guts, pressure, and seriousness is stressful and inefficient.

The manager who is able to maintain a sense of humor and to lighten the mental load of his colleagues will always have a motivated, happy team.

A sense of humor is a mark of intelligence. That is a quality desired in corporate presidents.

• LXVII •

Treat Your Family as Your Number One Client

*I*t is very easy to let your business career monopolize all your time and energy. The more action-oriented you become, the more there is to do. But to force your spouse and children into second place is a mistake.

You need the support of your family. It will help you in your career. You need an enthusiastic spouse who understands that some sacrifice is necessary. Your family must be an ally in your future plans.

Put your family on your calendar. Schedule as many soccer games as possible. Schedule vacations. Leave work early if you are taking your children trick-or-treating. Put family activities on your "To Do" list. Give them high priority. Quality time with your family will reward you a thousandfold.

When your spouse or children speak to you, put down the newspaper or book or mute the TV, and turn and look at them while they are speaking. You will strengthen that relationship and practice your listening skills at the same time. It is also a very polite thing to do.

Respond to your family as you do to your job, or to that big, important client.

• LXVIII •

No Goals, No Glory

*I*n hockey and soccer you need goals to win. A goal is the result of successful effort. No goals, no win, no glory. In business, no goals, no glory. In life, no goals, no glory.

You must set goals for yourself. The time management books insist goal setting is the first step in getting control over time. Goals shape your plans, direct your energies, and focus your resources.

You must write down your goals in your idea notebook (see chapter IX). You should have at least two sets of goals: one set for your business career and one set for your life. Your goals should have twenty-five-, ten-, five-, and one-year timetables. Your one-year goals should be broken down into twelve monthly steps. The month should be parceled into weekly steps.

You must create a yearly, monthly, weekly, and daily "To Do" list. On your "To Do" list write the things you have to do to reach your goals. On your daily "To Do" list, put some action that will get you closer to your long-range goals. This will keep you targeted.

If you don't have goals, you won't get them.

Goals beget goals.

• LXIX •

Always Remember
Your Subordinates' Spouses

A business career asks much of a person. Your success very much depends on the contribution of the people on your team. The easier you can make the burden of working, the farther your people can carry the load. A spouse can help or hurt. He or she can understand and be supportive or can nag and complain. He or she can make it easy for your colleague to work extra hours or to travel. Or the spouse can scuttle the whole effort.

The spouse is an important potential ally for the corporation; or frightfully, a virulent enemy.

This is such common sense, but the spouse is often forgotten, left out by the corporation.

Don't forget your people's families. When you get a chance, thank them personally for their support. When people are at a national sales meeting, send the spouse flowers. When you're on the road and a colleague wants or feels obligated to take you out to dinner be sure to invite the spouse as well.

Arrange an occasional "weekend for two" for a job well done.

Keep the spouse in mind. Everyone will be a little happier.

• LXX •

See the Job through
the Salespeople's Eyes

One of the oldest truisms of business is "Nothing happens until somebody sells something." Accountants won't count, manufacturers won't make, and managers won't manage . . . until and unless someone sells something. Very few products sell themselves. Most have to be sold. Someone has to get the order, get the product on the shelf, get the customer to spend money. Selling is key to the enterprise.

No matter what your function in the corporation, no matter what kind of a corporation, and regardless of the product or service, you must see the job through the salesperson's eyes. He or she is face-to-face and belly-to-belly with the customer. He hears the customer complaints. He receives the rejection.

Spend time in the field. Sell if you can. Travel with the salespeople. Make calls. Attend sales meetings. Conduct training sessions. Learn what goes on out there.

This will earn you credentials with the sales force, always a powerful constituency in any corporation. It will earn your spurs with sales management, always a powerful group in a corporation. You will know what motivates and demotivates the salespeople. You will have knowledge of customers, and that knowledge is a source of great power.

Work the trenches, and the trenches will work for you.

• LXXI •

Be a Very Tough
"Heller Seller"

You have to learn to sell like hell. Whether you want your department staff to work on Saturday, or you want your boss's approval on your latest scheme, or you want the plum project, you have to get the order. There are a million books on selling. Read some. You must become a tough, get-the-order salesperson.

To be a salesperson who sells, you do not have to have an outgoing personality or a glib line. You have to do the following:

1. Determine your "customer's" needs
2. Determine how your "product" will satisfy your customer's needs.
3. Develop an unshakable attitude of persistence and tenacity.
4. Make the "sales call."
5. Ask for the order.
6. Be prepared to make as many sales calls as are necessary to get the order.

Persistent and tenacious salespeople know that the numbers are in their favor. They know that 25 percent of all sales closes are made simply by asking for the order. They know that 75 percent of all sales closes are made on the fourth or subsequent call. They know that 90 percent of all salespeople never ask for the order. They know that 95 percent of all sales interviews are really conversation or entertainment, not selling. They know, therefore, that there is little competition for the persistent and tenacious salesperson. They know that making more calls and asking for the order is the formula for success.

Persistence, tenacity, attitude. The "heller sellers" have it.

• LXXII •

Don't Be an Empire Builder

Many managers mistakenly think that having the biggest budget or the most people reporting to them is a guarantee to getting the top job. Actually it is the manager who gets the job done with less—less people and less money—who is most needed by the corporation.

Never complain that you are expected to do more than your budget enables. Don't be the manager who constantly needs to hire people and is always adding to his department. Don't use the lack of resources as an excuse.

Forget the empire. Promotions and power go to producers, not to people administrators.

Push Products, Not Paper

*M*odern corporations are caught in a terrible dilemma. They need to streamline procedures and cut the "bureaucratic creep."* They need innovation and prudent risk-taking. They need entrepreneurship. Corporations need to spend all their resources—money, time, people,

---

*Bureaucratic creep describes the incremental growth of red tape in organizations . . . rules, useless forms, external task forces, old policies, and so on.

and plant—against the marketplace. But corporations drift to administration and paper.

Corporations are afraid of internal entrepreneurial spirit. They can't handle the personalities that build businesses. Most managers can't deal with the informal, antipolicy, antiprocedure style of idea people and business builders. Corporations want monthly reports, detailed expense accounts, personnel reviews on form paper, telephone logs, quarterly reports, year-end reports, one-hundred-page annual business plans, contingency plans, and hundreds of other energy- and time-draining requirements, none of which ring the cash register.

Do not get paper-trapped. Do not accept your corporation's paper handcuffs. Monthly reports are stupid. They are long, boring, late, and examples of creative writing in ancient history. Don't write any. If they insist, rotate the authorship among everyone on your staff. Everyone. Each person should write what they want. Don't encourage the report writer to copy anyone (saves copying and reading time). Don't bother reading them yourself.

Also don't write memos that rehash a meeting everyone just attended, trip reports (sophisticated expense account and job justifiers), or anything that does not directly improve your company.

• LXXIV •

To Teach Is to Learn
and to Lead

Always accept the chance to make a training presentation in your company. No matter what your job is you can improve your company by teaching others what you do (and what your staff does), why you do it, how you do it, and anything connected with your responsibility. If you're in finance or labor relations teach the new salesperson about finance or labor relations. If you are responsible for advertising or market research teach manufacturing people the ins and outs of television commercials and designing customer questionnaires.

If you have to teach you will prepare your presentation. Your preparation requires homework, organization, synthesis, and practice. The necessary study and discipline will help you master and add to your knowledge.

Good preparation and practice will produce a good presentation. A good presentation will earn you a company-wide reputation as an expert in your job. You will also become familiar with many people in other areas of the company. You will create strong circles of influence.

Teaching will improve your ability to articulate why your responsibility is critical to the company. Your audiences will come to believe that you are critical to the company.

• LXXV •

Do Not Get Discouraged by the Idea Killers

Companies are filled with idea killers. The idea killers come in all personalities, job titles, shapes, and sizes. The idea killers say things such as "we've tried that before," "management won't buy it," "we can't afford it," and a hundred other antirisk statements. One of the most common antiaction shots is the insufferable "it won't work." This is particularly frustrating because it usually comes from people both senior and experienced in the company. The young people who don't know that something can't be done get frustrated. The do-nothings who work at fulfilling their prophecy nourish the status quo.

During the oil embargoes of the 1970s, and the subsequent pressure to increase the miles-per-gallon efficiencies of cars, one of the major auto-makers told its senior engineers to drastically reduce the weight of cars. The senior engineers, imprisoned in their old ways, said making lighter cars couldn't be done, was too expensive, presented safety problems. So the car company hired lots of young, inexperienced engineers. The new engineers took hundreds of pounds of unnecessary weight off their cars. They just didn't know any better.

Don't give in. Don't let up. Idea people build businesses. Builders get to the top. Don't let the idea killers whittle you into mediocrity. Think boldly. Execute enthusiastically. Battle the inertia in the company. A little success will attract contributors and supporters from every corner of the company.

Consider the idea killers as a positive, as an incentive. Treat their negativism as a reason to do more homework. Work harder on the things necessary to make your idea work.

EPILOGUE

Thank you for reading this book. Now, reopen your book to one or two random pages. Put your finger on a section and do what is written.

You will be further on your way to becoming CEO.

ABOUT THE AUTHOR

Jeffrey J. Fox is the founder of Fox & Co., Inc., a premier marketing consulting company, serving over sixty companies in sixty industries and headquartered in Avon, Connecticut. Prior to starting Fox & Co., Mr. Fox was VP of Marketing and Corporate VP of Loctite Corporation. He was also Director of Marketing for the wine division of Pillsbury, and held various senior marketing posts at Heublein, Inc., including Director of New Products. Fox is the winner of *Sales and Marketing Management* magazine's Oustanding Marketer Award and the National Industrial Distributors Award as the Nation's Best Industrial Marketer. A graduate of Harvard Business School, he is the subject of a Harvard Business School case study that is rated one of the top one hundred case studies and is thought to be the most widely taught marketing case in the world. He has been featured in *The Wall Street Journal*, *Business Marketing*, and numerous other publications, and he is a member of the Board of Trustees at Trinity College in Hartford. He lives in Connecticut.

**Vermilion books are available from all good bookshops or call our mail order hotline number on:
01206 255 800**

Postage and packing is free.